# Spelling, Punctuation & Grammar Made Easy

**Key Stage 2**
**AGES 10-11**

**Author** Claire White
**Consultant** Amy O'Connor

**DK**

# Certificate

Congratulations to

......................................
(write your name here)

for successfully
finishing this book.

## GOOD JOB!

You're a star.

**AGES 10-11**

**Key Stage 2**

Date

......................

 | Penguin Random House

**DK London**
**Editors** Elizabeth Blakemore,
Jolyon Goddard
**Senior Art Editor** Ann Cannings
**Managing Editor** Christine Stroyan
**Managing Art Editor** Anna Hall
**Senior Production Editor** Andy Hilliard
**Senior Production Controller** Jude Crozier
**Jacket Design Development Manager** Sophia MTT
**Publisher** Andrew Macintyre
**Associate Publishing Director** Liz Wheeler
**Art Director** Karen Self
**Publishing Director** Jonathan Metcalf

**DK Delhi**
**Project Editor** Neha Ruth Samuel
**Editor** Nandini Gupta
**Designers** Rashika Kachroo, Radhika Kapoor
**Managing Editors** Soma B. Chowdhury, Kingshuk Ghoshal
**Managing Art Editors** Ahlawat Gunjan, Govind Mittal
**DTP Designers** Vishal Bhatia, Anita Yadav,
Rakesh Kumar, Harish Aggarwal
**Senior Jacket Designer** Suhita Dharamjit
**Jackets Editorial Coordinator** Priyanka Sharma

This edition published in 2020
First published in Great Britain in 2015 by
Dorling Kindersley Limited
DK, One Embassy Gardens, 8 Viaduct Gardens, London, SW11 7BW

The authorised representative in the EEA is
Dorling Kindersley Verlag GmbH. Arnulfstr. 124,
80636 Munich, Germany

Copyright © 2015, 2020 Dorling Kindersley Limited
A Penguin Random House Company
11 10 9 8 7
007–272763–Apr/2020

Printed and bound in China

## For the curious
**www.dk.com**

MIX
Paper from
responsible sources
FSC™ C018179

This book was made with Forest Stewardship
Council™ certified paper – one small step
in DK's commitment to a sustainable future.
For more information go to
www.dk.com/our-green-pledge

# Contents

This chart lists all of the topics in the book. When you have completed each page, colour in a star in the correct box. When you have finished the book, sign and date the certificate.

# ★ Silent consonants

Some consonants are silent in the spelling of a word. They are written, but not pronounced. The secret silent consonants lurk where you cannot hear them. You will never know they are there, unless you know how to spell the word. For example: the **b** in **limb** and the **w** in **sword** are both silent consonants.

Look at the words in the word bank carefully. Then, fill in each silent-consonant box.

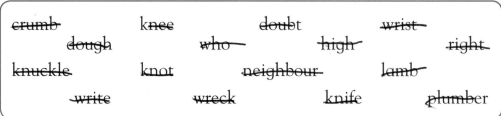

crumb          knee          doubt          wrist

   dough          who          high          right

knuckle          knot          neighbour          lamb

   write          wreck          knife          plumber

**silent B**

crumb
lamb
daubt
plumber

**silent W**

Write
Wreck
Wrist
Who

**silent GH**

high
olough
right
neighbour

**silent K**

Knee
Knife
Knot
Knuckle

**FACTS**

> A **root word** is usually a complete word in itself, such as **order** or **break**. You can, however, make a new word by adding a prefix or a suffix to a root word. For example: **dis** + **order** = **disorder** and **break** + **able** = **breakable**.

Remove the prefix or suffix from each of the words below to find the root word.

| Word | Root word |
|------|-----------|
| misbehave | mis behave |
| sincerely | sincere |
| training | semi semi train |
| semicircle | dis dis circle |
| disagree | in in agree |
| intensify | sub tensisy |
| submarine | dis marine |
| disappear | appear |
| equipped | ed equip |
| lengthen | able length |
| drinkable | pre drink |
| preschool | school |

Now pick any two pairs of words from the chart above. Write four sentences, each including one of the words you picked.

My brother allways misbehaves.

Im a green belt in training

Sea water isn't drinkable

My homework book disappeared

# Prefixes

A **prefix** is a group of letters added to the beginning of a root word to change its meaning. For example: **dis** + **approve** = **disapprove**.

Match each prefix to its meaning below. **Hint**: think about the words you know that use these prefixes and their meanings.

| | |
|---|---|
| **dis** | again or back |
| **de** | reverses the meaning of the verb |
| **mis** | badly or wrongly |
| **re** | do the opposite of |

Choose and write the correct prefix from the exercise above for each of these root words.

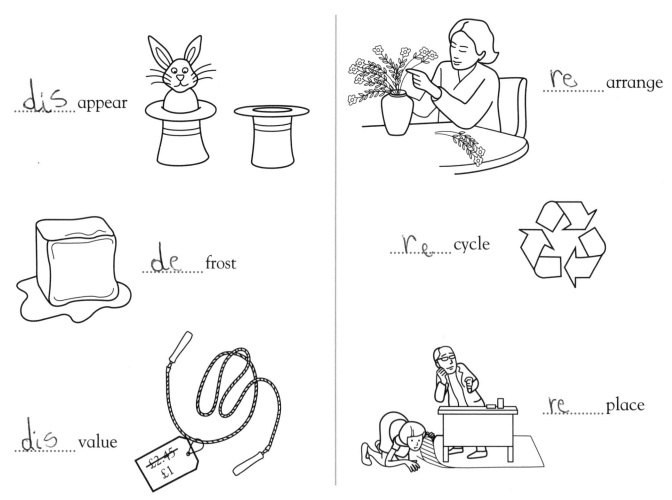

*dis* appear

*re* arrange

*de* frost

*re* cycle

*dis* value

*re* place

A **suffix** is a group of letters added to the end of a root word to change its meaning. For example: **walk** + **ing** = **walking**. Suffixes are not complete words and cannot be used on their own in a sentence.

Change the nouns and adjectives into verbs by adding one of these suffixes: **ate**, **ify**, **ise** or **en**.

| Nouns/Adjectives | Verbs |
| --- | --- |
| standard | .......................... |
| straight | Sraighten |
| note | notify |
| elastic | elastisy |
| deep | deepen |
| hyphen | hyhenate |
| apology | apologise |
| dead | deaden |
| pure | purify |
| loose | loosen |
| glory | glorify |

What do you notice about the root words above ending in **y** and **e**?

..............................................................................................................

Choose two verbs from the exercise above and write sentences using them.

~~that~~ You need aflogise for your behavine.

that line ~~tin~~ need To be straightened

An **antonym** is a word that has an opposite meaning to another word.

For example:

**forget** means the opposite of **remember**

Write an antonym for each of these words.

| | |
|---|---|
| strong | ................................ |
| first | ................................ |
| near | ................................ |
| youngest | ................................ |
| clean | ................................ |
| good | ................................ |
| question | ................................ |
| dark | ................................ |

Now try these. Read each complete word and then fill in the missing letters of the word beside it to make an antonym.

shorten       len___en

hope       des___r

antonym       sy___m

vertical       horiz___al

compulsory       volun___y

optional       nec___ary

Antonyms are sometimes made by adding a prefix.

For example:  edible  inedible

Choose from the prefixes **un**, **in** and **dis** to make each word mean the opposite.
Write the antonym in the space provided.

| Word | Antonym |
|---|---|
| safe | ................................. |
| expensive | ................................. |
| willing | ................................. |
| agree | ................................. |
| complete | ................................. |
| comfort | ................................. |

Complete these sentences using the correct antonym.
**Hint:** look at the words in italics and use the prefixes you have just learned.

The instructor was clearly not *qualified* to teach the class;
therefore, he was ................................. .

At first the magician's assistant was *visible* and then after
he said the magic words she was ................................. !

I *like* to munch on apples, but I have a strong
................................. for apple pie.

**FACTS**

There are lots of different types of punctuation, but it is very important to use the correct punctuation in the correct places. Otherwise, the meaning of a sentence may not be clear and will confuse the reader.

Eloise sometimes forgets to use the correct punctuation in her writing. Read her sentences and add the corrections where necessary. Use the key below to add missing punctuation marks. Where a small letter needs to be capital, add a star (*) next to it.

| " " | inverted commas/speech marks |
|---|---|
| . | full stop |
| , | comma |

I want to go to the beach!  shouted Chloe

is that a clown?  asked Freya

it was time to go  It had been a hard day

I think that is hilarious  laughed Leon

That really hurt!  yelled  leah

it has all been worth it

daniel bought oranges  apples  bread and milk

I am going on holiday soon

Now write a sentence demonstrating the use of each type of punctuation.

...........................................................................................................................

...........................................................................................................................

Properly punctuated written English ensures that sentences can be understood clearly and avoids ambiguity, or double meaning.

Match each of the punctuation marks first to its name and then to its definition.

| ; | apostrophe | This mark sometimes links two or more simple sentences that share a common theme. |
| : | hyphen | This mark is used to show that an example, explanation or list is to follow. |
| - | colon | This mark is used to link words or parts of words. |
| , | semi-colon | This mark is used to show possession or a contraction. |

Now read the sentences below carefully and fill in the correct punctuation marks.
**Hint:** you can also use other punctuation marks that you have already learned.

There s a reason why I didn t go to Adam s party
I didn t have a fancy dress costume

Is this café self service

It s a really exciting day today  you can tell it s her birthday

Is this book yours   the teacher asked
No  it s Zoe s  I replied

Isobel had an X ray of her arm

Don t do that

Punctuation can be quite complicated and confusing. It is helpful to read written work aloud to help you decide where the punctuation marks should go.

A **colon** (:) is used before a list of words, phrases or clauses. Here is an example. The following were in the boot of the car: beach balls, buckets and spades.

A **semi-colon** (;) is used in a list to separate items that are longer than one or two words. Here is an example. There were several new features in the garden: a pond; a sensory trail along the path; a willow dome; and a bench area for picnics. **Note**: unlike commas, a semi-colon is used before the final item in the list.

Look at the items in the boot of the car below. Write a sentence using a colon to punctuate the list of the items you see.

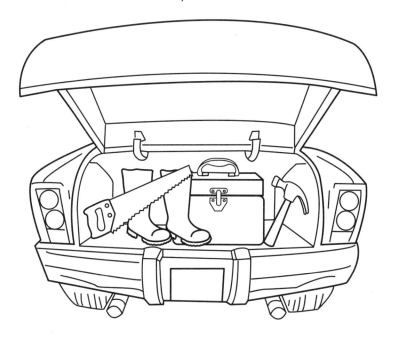

..........................................................................................................................................................

..........................................................................................................................................................

Read the sentence below. It lists a number of items you might find in a garden. Add semi-colons in the right places to separate the items in the list. **Remember**: semi-colons are used to separate items that are longer than one or two words.

These are the items in my shed: a spade to dig the soil

a watering can to water the plants  a pair of gloves

and a set of ceramic flower pots.

FACTS

Colons and semi-colons are also used in bulleted lists. A colon is used before the list begins and semi-colons are used to separate the various items. A full stop is used at the end of the list because it is also the end of the sentence.
Here is an example.

Equipment required for PE:
- shorts;
- T-shirt;
- trainers.

Think of all the things you might need to pack if you were going away on holiday. Then make a list of the items using a colon and semi-colons.

.................................................................................................

- ..............................................................

- ..............................................................

- ..............................................................

- ..............................................................

- ..............................................................

- ..............................................................

Next time you need to make a list, punctuate it with colons and semi-colons. It will look pretty impressive!

See if you can spot the use of colons and semi-colons in newspapers and magazines.

FACTS

An **ellipsis** (…) is often used by a writer when he or she wants the reader to fill in the details. Ellipses can also indicate an unfinished thought, a pause or a nervous or awkward silence in writing. For example: **I knew I'd seen his face before…** Using an ellipsis is a good way of building suspense or mystery in your writing.

Complete each of these sentences by adding words and then ending with an ellipsis.

The three friends ........................................................

The door ........................................................

The castle ........................................................

Behind them ........................................................

Through the forest ........................................................

It was a bone-chilling evening ........................................................

Finish writing this opening paragraph of a story. **Note:** use at least one ellipsis to add an element of suspense or mystery.

Daniel and Leah walked slowly towards ........

the trees. They were excited to have moved ....

house and be living so close to such ..........

a huge forest. .......................................

........................................................

........................................................

........................................................

........................................................

........................................................

# Parenthesis: using brackets

**Parenthesis** is the use of brackets in a sentence to give more information, explain a difficult word, show thoughts or emphasise a point. For example: the girls **(who were very excited)** couldn't wait to get to the zoo.
**Parenthesis** (plural: **parentheses**) is also another word for **bracket**.

Remove the parentheses from these sentences and rearrange them to create two separate sentences.

Merlin and Doodles (our much-loved pet cats) were fighting when Zoe arrived home.

.................................................................................................................................

.................................................................................................................................

The headphones (red and black) were very expensive.

.................................................................................................................................

.................................................................................................................................

The boots (made of black leather) were scuffed and dirty.

.................................................................................................................................

.................................................................................................................................

For each of these pairs of sentences, rewrite them as one sentence that uses parenthesis.

The graph shows the popularity of each football team. The graph is on the previous page.

.................................................................................................................................

.................................................................................................................................

The Eiffel Tower is one of the most iconic landmarks in the world. The Eiffel Tower is found in Paris.

.................................................................................................................................

.................................................................................................................................

**Bullet points** are used to highlight important information within a piece of text, so that a reader can identify the key points and extract information quickly.

**Guidelines for using bullet points:**

- The text introducing the bullet points should end with a colon;

- If the text that follows the bullet point is not a complete sentence, it doesn't need to start with a capital letter;

- If the text following the bullet point is a complete sentence, it should begin with a capital letter;

- You can end the text following each bullet point with a semi-colon, no punctuation at all, or a full stop if it is a complete sentence. The text following the last bullet point, however, should always end with a full stop.

Here is a picture of Flib-Flob the Alien. Write bullet points to describe him. The first one has been done for you.

This alien:

- has large oval eyes;

- ...............................................................................

- ...............................................................................

- ...............................................................................

Use bullet points to make a list of the main points of a book you have recently read.

The main points are:

- ...............................................................................

- ...............................................................................

- ...............................................................................

- ...............................................................................

See if you can find examples of bullet points in newspapers and magazines.

# Apostrophe to show possession

FACTS

As well as being used in contractions (such as **we'll** and **shouldn't**), apostrophes are used to show possession, or ownership, as in **the peacock's feathers** or **in one month's time**. Apostrophes showing possession can go in two places, depending on the number of possessors. For one possessor, the apostrophe is placed before an added **s**, as in **the cat's food**. This refers to food belonging to one cat. For more than one possessor, the apostrophe is placed at the end of the plural word, as in **the cats' food**. This refers to food belonging to more than one cat.

There are exceptions to these rules. For example: singular words that end in **s** can end with just an apostrophe (') or an apostrophe and **s** ('s).
For example: **Charles' birthday** and **Charles's birthday** are both acceptable.

Draw a line to match each phrase with apostrophes to the number of brothers and friends it refers to. Think carefully before you start.

my brother's
friend's clothes

one brother with
more than one friend


my brother's
friends' clothes

more than one brother
and their friends


my brothers'
friend's clothes

one brother and
his friend


my brothers'
friends' clothes

more than one brother
and their friend

# ★ Homophones

A **homophone** is a word that is pronounced, or sounds, the same as another word but has a different spelling and meaning. For example: **sun** and **son**.

Read the passage below and underline the homophones that you think have been spelled incorrectly. Then make a list of the correct spellings in the space under the passage.

It was late one wintry Sunday knight. A young elf, with an outrageously long beard and matted hare, was sitting on a toadstool eating magic serial. His friends thought it strange that he liked to eat serial at knight, but even stranger were the contents of the serial! The bowl, witch was full to the brim, contained currents, a peace of would, the herb time and the stumpy tale of a wild bare! The elf didn't really care weather his friends thought it strange. He simply ignored them when they wood pass and stair.

...................................        ...................................

...................................        ...................................

...................................        ...................................        ...................................

...................................        ...................................        ...................................

...................................        ...................................        ...................................

The spelling rhyme "I before E except after C" is well known, but it does not always apply.

**The rule does apply:**

• when the letters together make a long **e** sound, as in **deceit** and **shield**.

**The rule does not apply:**

• when the letters together make a long **a** sound, as in **sleigh**;

• when using the plural form for words ending in **cy**, as in **pregnancies**;

• when the letters **i** and **e** are pronounced as separate vowels in words, as in **science**.

Write the missing **ie** or **ei** in the space provided below. **Remember**: think carefully about the rule and its exceptions before completing the words.

| | | |
|---|---|---|
| c__ling | polic__s | shr__k |
| f__ld | pric__r | soc__ty |
| fr__ght | rec__pt | th__f |
| frequenc__s | rec__ve | vacanc__s |
| n__ghbour | r__gn | v__l |
| p__ce | rel__f | w__ght |

Can you think of any exceptions? Here are some clues:

A part of our diet .....................................

Eerie or strange .....................................

To grab hold .....................................

FACTS

You use **direct speech** to write down exactly what a person says. You must enclose the words being said within inverted commas.
For example: **"I have no idea what is going on!" said Mrs Wilson.**

Write down what the aliens Bee-Bee and Bo-Bo are saying in the speech bubbles as direct speech. Make sure you put inverted commas around their words, followed by **asked Bo-Bo** or **replied Bee-Bee**.
**Remember**: start a new line each time a new person, or character, speaks.

You use **reported speech** to write what has been said, but you do not use the exact spoken words. You report it in your own words as the writer. For example: **Mrs White said that she was so pleased with her class.**

Imagine you are writing a report about the new aliens landing on the planet where Bo-Bo and Bee-Bee live. Using reported speech, write next to the aliens what they said about the new visitors.

I could not believe my eyes!

..................................................................................
..................................................................................
..................................................................................
..................................................................................

..................................................................................
..................................................................................
..................................................................................
..................................................................................

Will the new aliens take over our planet?

I think they will be friendly, like us.

..................................................................................
..................................................................................
..................................................................................
..................................................................................

Now try writing a report of an event you have been involved in, such as a birthday celebration or a sporting event at school.

**FACTS**

**Formal speech** is used in official writing and situations, such as legal documents, news reports, business letters and official speeches. **Informal speech** is used in everyday conversations and personal letters or emails.

Read the three different letters numbered 1, 2 and 3. Then, write the corresponding numbers in the three small boxes at the bottom of the page, in order from most formal to least formal (informal).

**1**

Dear Kayte,

I have been to the beach today and the weather was great. I went swimming! I hope to see you soon,

Lots of love,
Claire

**2**

To Whom it May Concern,

Today I went to a beautiful beach on the south coast. We were lucky that the weather was really good for this time of year. We also had the opportunity to go swimming, which meant we all got some well-needed exercise. I look forward to hearing from you.

Kind regards,
Ms C White

**3**

Hi Kayte!

Been to beach. Great weather. Went swimming.

See you soon.
Claire

Most formal                                                    Least formal

 ⟶  ⟶ ⬚

Formal and informal writing and speech differ from each other in tone and structure.

Write a letter to your friend telling him or her about your last holiday.
Think about whether you will write the letter in formal or informal speech.

# ★ Points of view

A story or any other type of writing can be written from different points of view.
If it is written from the writer's point of view, it is said to be in the first person.
For example: **I saw a spaceship in the sky.**
When the point of view is that of an outside observer, it is said to be in the
third person. For example: **Sophie saw a spaceship in the sky.**

Read each sentence below carefully. Write **first person** or **third person** next to
each, depending on the point of view.

Every summer, I look forward to the warm evenings. ...........................................

The hedgehog curled up inside the hollow log.
He got himself ready for the long, sleepy winter. ...............................

When I heard the birds chirping, I knew it was the
break of dawn. ...............................

I feel proud of everything my daughter has achieved. ...............................

Katy knew how well she had done at Irish dancing
and was full of pride. ...............................

The hairdresser asked Alena, "Just the usual cut today?"
Alena wondered if she should try something new. ...............................

I am going on holiday soon. ...............................

Write two sentences: one in the first person and another in the third person.

.......................................................................................

.......................................................................................

**Personification** is a figure of speech in which non-human things are described as having human characteristics, as in **the blushing sun** or **the angry storm**. This type of **figurative language** is often used in poetry. It can help create a vivid picture in the mind of the reader.

Read this poem. Extract the lines using personification and rewrite them below.

**It's Coming!**

I can smell it in the air; I can feel it in my bones,
It's coming!
Light creeps away,
Dark is dawning on us,
Raindrops frown as they start to pummel the colourless pavement,
It's coming!
Whispering trees dance in the howling wind,
It's grey gravel gravitating downwards from the stormy skies above,
It's coming!
Hail starts to break through the thick murky cotton wool,
Cold crystal tears streaming down pale cheek,
It's coming!
Streaks of light strike the innocent houses below.
The tempest is here.

Alisha Charlton (age 11)

......................................................................................................................................

......................................................................................................................................

......................................................................................................................................

Now match each season to its personification below.

Spring                              His icy cold fingers cling to the branches.

Summer                           His light steps bring new life to everything he touches.

Autumn                           Her skin is dry and wrinkled, lifeless and bare.

Winter                             Her hair is a blaze of light, shedding warmth to
                                        those around her.

# ★ Exploring synonyms

FACTS

**Synonyms** are words with the same or similar meaning, such as **happy** and **content** or **ill** and **poorly**. Words that are synonyms of each other are said to be synonymous.

Draw a line to match each pair of synonyms below.

| | |
|---|---|
| buy | large |
| big | on |
| quickly | purchase |
| upon | speedily |

Write each of the words from the exercise above under one of these headings.

| Verb | Adjective | Adverb | Preposition |
|---|---|---|---|
| .......................... | .......................... | .......................... | .......................... |
| .......................... | .......................... | .......................... | .......................... |

Now think of a synonym to go with each of the adjectives below.

dangerous .....................................

small .....................................

clever .....................................

broad .....................................

wealthy .....................................

slender .....................................

Synonyms help improve your writing and make it more engaging. For instance, using synonyms of the word **said**, which is often overused, will make your writing more interesting. When doing this, think carefully about how the character is speaking and what is being said.

The characters below are saying something in a certain way. Think of a synonym for **said** that reflects the way they are speaking. Then, write the sentence using the synonym. The first one has been done for you.

| What is said | How it is said | Synonym and sentence |
| --- | --- | --- |
| "I am going to the Wizardland." | in a happy way | beamed<br><br>"I am going to the Wizardland!"<br><br>beamed the girl. |
| "They said I couldn't climb the magic tree." | in a sad way | |
| "It's not my fault!" | in a frightened way | |
| "This way, my lady." | as an answer | |

A **simple sentence** has one subject and one verb. For example: **Phoebe lives in France.**

A **compound sentence** has two main clauses, which could both stand on their own as separate sentences, joined by a connective. For example: **Phoebe lives in France, but I live in England.**

A **complex sentence** has a main clause and one or more subordinate clauses, joined by a connective. A subordinate clause contains a subject and a verb, but it needs to be attached to a main clause because it does not make much sense on its own. For example: **I first met Phoebe in Paris, where I lived as a small child.**

Study the picture below. Then write a simple, a compound and a complex sentence based on this picture.

**Simple sentence**

......................................................................................................................................

......................................................................................................................................

**Compound sentence**

......................................................................................................................................

......................................................................................................................................

**Complex sentence**

......................................................................................................................................

......................................................................................................................................

When a sentence has two clauses, a connective is used to join them together. The clauses may be two main clauses, making a compound sentence, or a main clause and a subordinate clause, making a complex sentence. Common connectives include **and**, **which**, **although**, **after**, **before** and **so**.

Read the sentences below. Draw one line under the main clause, two lines under the subordinate clause and a circle around the connective. Reread the opposite page to help you. The first one has been done for you.

I like apples (and) I like oranges.

I could go the beach or I could stay home.

Zoe wanted some new clothes, so she went shopping.

Peter took three biscuits, which he later gave to Isobel.

Before Zoe went to school, Isobel came round for breakfast.

Amy watched TV after she had finished her homework.

I tried to explain to Anna, although she didn't understand.

Non-fiction writing is based on facts and is different from stories, which come from an author's imagination. The following are all types of non-fiction writing: a retelling of real-life events; instructions; a technical explanation; an opinion or argument; a discussion; and a description of the characteristics of something. The chapters of non-fiction books can often be read in any order. Such books usually have a contents page, a glossary and an index.

Read this extract about the duck-billed platypus. Use the information to create a piece of non-fiction writing. Give your piece of writing a heading and, if you want, use bullet points to highlight the animal's key characteristics.

All animals are different, but platypuses are particularly unusual animals. They look like a mixture of many other animals. They have flat tails, like beavers. They have thick fur that is well suited to water, like otters. They have bills and webbed feet, like ducks. Their webbed feet have claws, so they are able to dig and swim. Platypuses are also unusual because they are venomous mammals. A male platypus can sting other creatures to defend himself. Finally, platypuses are one of the very few mammals that lay eggs.

...................................................................................................

...................................................................................................

...................................................................................................

...................................................................................................

...................................................................................................

...................................................................................................

...................................................................................................

...................................................................................................

FACTS

> **Onomatopoeia** is the formation of words that imitate the sound of the objects or actions to which they refer. For example: **crunch**, **hiccup**, **ha-ha**, **vroom** and animal noises, such as **moo**, **miaow** and **oink**, are all onomatopoeic words. It is a form of figurative language, like personification.

Read this poem. In the space provided below, list the onomatopoeic words the poet has used in the poem.

## Clocks

Ding, Dong, Ding, Dong!
The grandfather clocks aren't wrong.
The clocks' hands turn around,
Standing tall above the ground.
Ding, Dong, Ding, Dong!

Beep, Beep, Beep, Beep!
Says the stopwatch after his sleep.
He will stop at your every word.
That beep is what everyone heard.
Beep, Beep, Beep, Beep!

Bong, Bong, Bong, Bong!
Big Ben sounds like a gong.
Towering tall over London city,
Making citizens look so tiny.
Bong, Bong, Bong, Bong!

Tick, Tick, Tick, Tick!
Chimes the ongoing wall clock.
It will stay ticking forever.
When will it stop? Never!

Craig Robson (age 11)

......................................................

......................................................          ......................................................

......................................................          ......................................................

**FACTS**

Once you have learned the rules associated with spelling, including the use of prefixes and suffixes, it is easier to spell a range of words correctly. Another way to learn spelling is the look-cover-write-check method.

Follow the look-cover-write-check method, as shown below, to learn the spelling of the words listed on this page. If you are unsure of the meaning of any of these words, ask your parent to help you look them up in a dictionary.

**1.** Look (at the word)

**2.** Cover (the word)

**3.** Write (the word)

**4.** Check (to see if you got it right!)

| | | | |
|---|---|---|---|
| variety | ..................................... | disastrous | ..................................... |
| secretary | ..................................... | frequently | ..................................... |
| amateur | ..................................... | opportunity | ..................................... |
| prejudice | ..................................... | guarantee | ..................................... |
| recommend | ..................................... | profession | ..................................... |
| equipment | ..................................... | interfere | ..................................... |
| curiosity | ..................................... | yacht | ..................................... |
| hindrance | ..................................... | accompany | ..................................... |
| queue | ..................................... | lightning | ..................................... |
| temperature | ..................................... | nuisance | ..................................... |
| bargain | ..................................... | environment | ..................................... |